Modern Rudimental Swing Solos

for the Advanced Drummer

10300203

LUDWIG Masters
PUBLICATIONS

About the Composer

Charles Wilcoxon was born in Newark, Ohio on November 26, 1894. Early in life, he showed his talent and love for the drums, playing for hours on homemade drums made from whatever was at hand, and giving shows. To earn the money for his first drum set, Wilcoxon would deliver papers, run delivery errands for a furniture store, and perform farm yard chores around town. At 14, he joined the show *Spring Maid*, the equivalent to *My Fair Lady* of today on the vaudeville circuit.

After leaving the vaudeville theatre, Charles opened a drum shop and studio where he had a lathe and turned out custom made drum sticks, and taught percussion studies, his passion. While writing drum parts for each individual student, Charles decided to put his playing experience in book form, which became *Modern Rudimental Swing Solos for the Advanced Drummer*. *The All-American Drummer* was done by hand in six weeks. His next book was *Drum Method*, which he also used for his instructions. He went on to write such books as *Drummer On Parade With Street Beats*, *The Junior Drummer*, *Rolling in Rhythm*, *Drumming! Plus Hummin' a Tune*, and individual contest drum solos. He always said "Don't copy; be original," which is exactly what he was.

"The ability to teach is the rarest of gifts."

—Excerpts from an autobiography written by "Mrs. Charley"

The Open Stroke Roll

Closed Stroke Rolls

Single Paradiddle

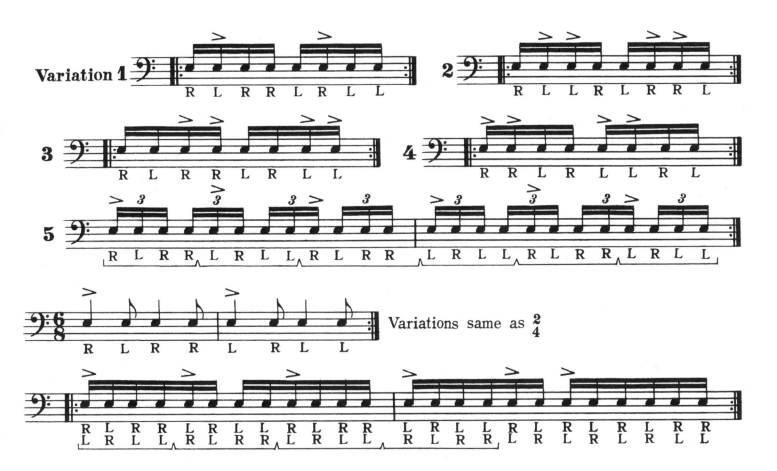

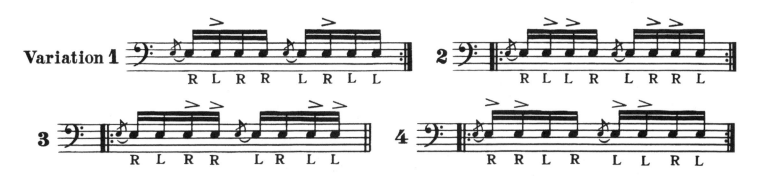

Flam Paradiddle

For greater variety of beats add various Flams to above single Paradiddle studies.

Double Paradiddle

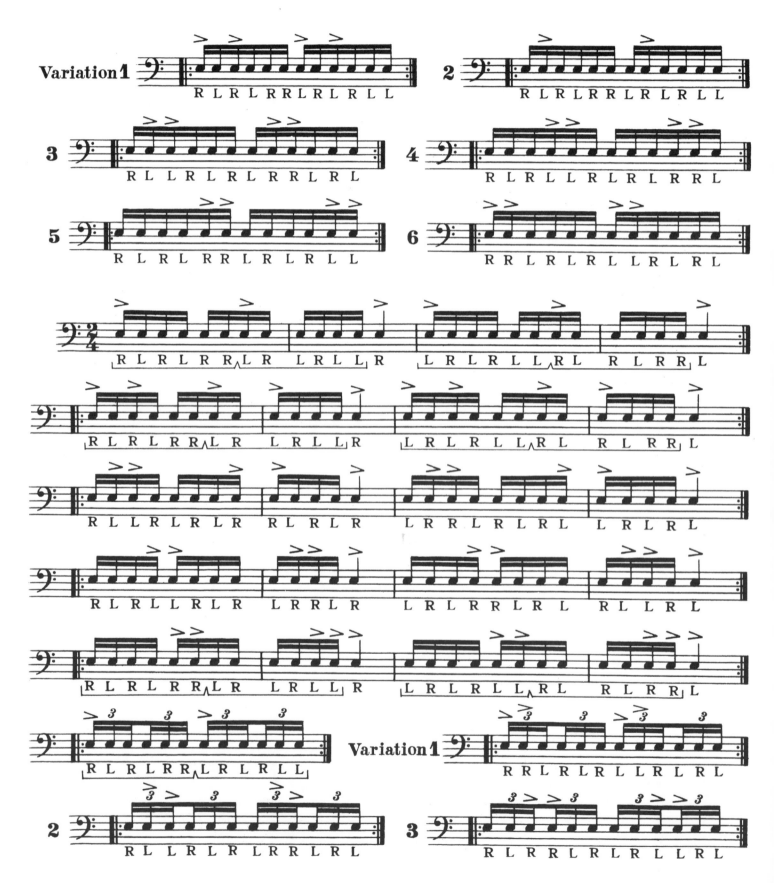

Flam Double Paradiddle

Note: For greater variety of beats, add Flams to DOUBLE PARADIDDLES (single)

Flam Tap

Flamacue

8

Flam Accent No. 1

Flam Accent No. 2

Single Drag

Version No. 1

Version No. 2

3 Stroke Ruff

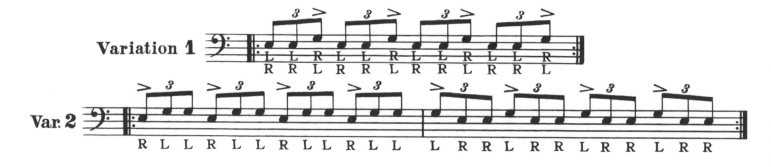

Double Drag

Single Ratamacue

Double Ratamacue

Triple Ratamacue

Drag Paradiddle No. 1

Drag Paradiddle No. 2

The Flam Paradiddle - Diddle

R L R R L L   L R L L R R

Variation 1

25th Rudiment

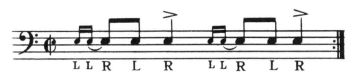

L L R L R   L L R L R

Version 1

Variation 1
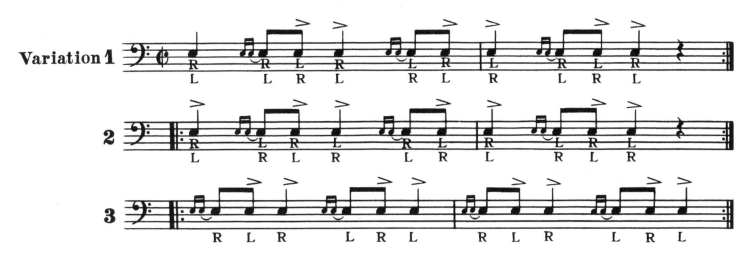

♩=150   50"

Dedicated to "Joe" Morello

Rolling In Rhythm

C. S. WILCOXON

Drum Solo

Dedicated to "Creight" Davies

The Flam Stomp

Drum - High hat
Bass Drum

C. S. WILCOXON

Rhythmania

Drum Solo

C. S. WILCOXON

Paradiddle Johnnie

Drum Solo

C. S. WILCOXON

Dedicated to Wilson Gebhardt

Swinging Accents

Drum Solo

C.S. WILCOXON

Dedicated to Olive Gresmer (Cleveland Plain Dealer)

Deep Central

Two Tom-Toms

C.S. WILCOXON

Dedicated to "Louie" Bellson

Roughing the Single Drag

Drum Solo

C.S.WILCOXON

Dedicated to American Legion Post No. 12, Elyria, Ohio

Elyria Four Stroke

Drum Solo

C.S. WILCOXON

Study In Accents

Drum Solo

C.S.WILCOXON

Dedicated to American Legion Post No. 30, Lorain, Ohio

Lorain Post Dug-Out

Drum Solo

C. S. WILCOXON

The Corn Belt Jive

Drum Solo

C.S. WILCOXON

Modern Flam Accents

Drum Solo

C. S. WILCOXON

The Flam Accent Fantasy

Drum Solo

C. S. WILCOXON

Dedicated to Fred Albright

The New Downfall

Drum Solo

C.S. WILCOXON

Dedicated to Ormand Downs

Heating The Rudiments

Drum Solo

C. S. WILCOXON

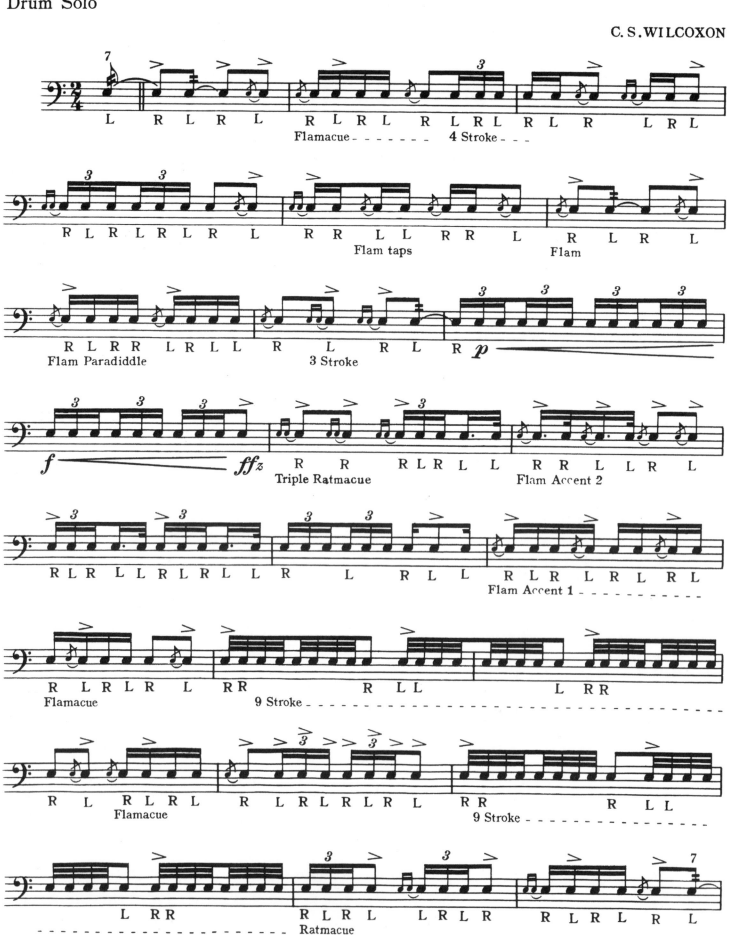

Old Sue

Drum Solo

C. S. WILCOXON

The Rhumba

Bongo-Drums
or 2 Tom-Toms

C.S.WILCOXON

Dedicated to George Way

Home Cookin'

Drum Solo

C.S. WILCOXON

Dedicated to GENE KRUPA. (The Dean of "Swing")

Ubangi Serenade

Solo for two Tom-Toms

C. S. WILCOXON

Sweet Susan

Drum Solo

C. S. WILCOXON

Shots
Right Stick on Left

Dedicated to J.C. McLeland

The Yankee Doodle Stomp

Drum Solo

C. S. WILCOXON

Mr. J. Edward Heeps

Drum Solo

C. S. WILCOXON

The Tiger

Drum Solo

C. S. WILCOXON

Loosen Up

C. S. WILCOXON

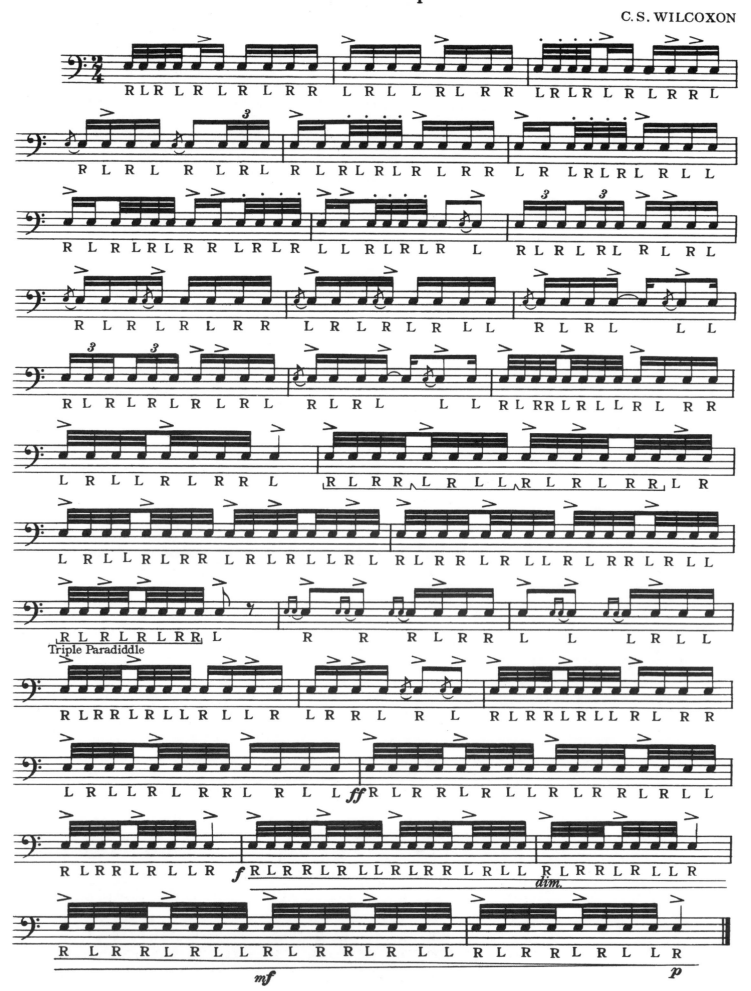

Dedicated to James Lamb

The Scotty

Drum Solo

C.S. WILCOXON

Dedicated to "Tommy" Thompson -- Boston Orchestra

Rudimental Jam

C.S. WILCOXON

Drum Solo

The Spanish Three Eight

C.S. WILCOXON

Dedicated to (Chas. Owen) University of Michigan

Swinging the "26"

Drum Solo

C.S.WILCOXON

Dedicated to Charles Botterill. (Mantovani Orch.)

Three Camps

Drum Solo

Variations by
C. S. WILCOXON

Three Camps in Paradiddles

C.S.WILCOXON

Variation 1

Three Camps In Ratamacues

C.S.WILCOXON

Variation 2

Dedicated to Robert Matson Cleveland Orchestra

Battin Em' Out

Drum Solo

C.S. WILCOXON